F

USAIN BOLT

OLYMPIC SPRINTER

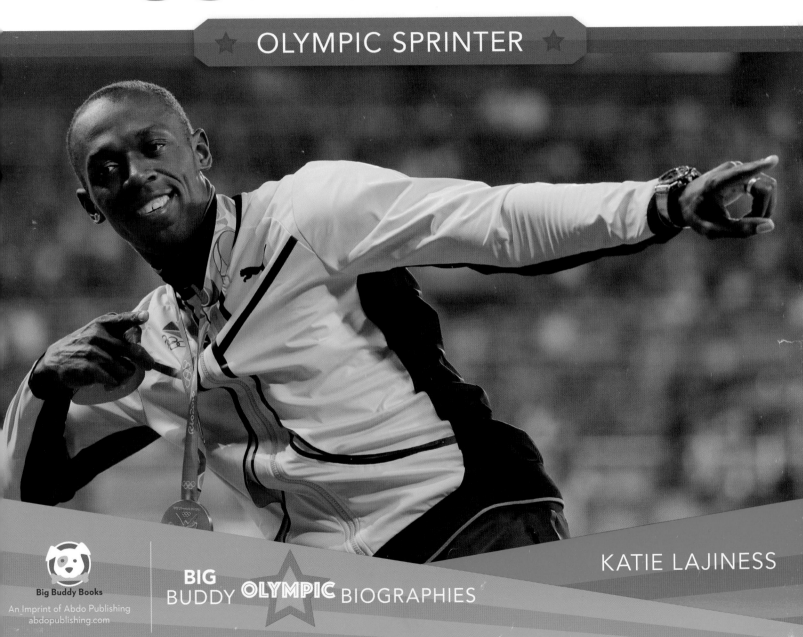

KATIE LAJINESS

Big Buddy Books
An Imprint of Abdo Publishing
abdopublishing.com

BIG BUDDY OLYMPIC BIOGRAPHIES

abdopublishing.com

Published by Abdo Publishing, a division of ABDO, PO Box 398166, Minneapolis, Minnesota 55439.
Copyright © 2017 by Abdo Consulting Group, Inc. International copyrights reserved in all countries.
No part of this book may be reproduced in any form without written permission from the publisher.
Big Buddy Books™ is a trademark and logo of Abdo Publishing.

Printed in the United States of America, North Mankato, Minnesota.
102016
012017

Cover Photo: ASSOCIATED PRESS
Interior Photos: ASSOCIATED PRESS (pp. 6, 11, 13, 14, 19, 23); Evan Agostini/Invision/AP (p. 27);
   KGC-146/STAR MAX/IPx/AP (p. 29); Shutterstock (p. 9); Sipa USA via AP (pp. 21, 25); ZUMA Press,
   Inc./Alamy Stock Photo (pp. 5, 17, 23).

Coordinating Series Editor: Tamara L. Britton
Graphic Design: Jenny Christensen

Publisher's Cataloging-in-Publication Data

Names: Lajiness, Katie, author.
Title: Usain Bolt / by Katie Lajiness.
Description: Minneapolis, MN : Abdo Publishing, 2017. | Series: Big buddy
   Olympic biographies | Includes bibliographical references and index.
Identifiers: LCCN 2016953146 | ISBN 9781680785517 (lib. bdg.) |
   ISBN 9781680785791 (ebook)
Subjects: LCSH: Bolt, Usain, 1986- --Juvenile literature. | Track and field
   athletes--Jamaica--Biography--Juvenile literature. | Olympic athletes--
   Jamaica--Biography--Juvenile literature. | Olympic Games (31st : 2016 : Rio
   de Janeiro, Brazil)
Classification: DDC 796.42/092 [B]--dc23
LC record available at http://lccn.loc.gov/2016953146

CONTENTS

RECORD BREAKER

Usain Bolt is a famous **sprinter**. He has won races at the Olympics and world **championships**.

Usain has won nine Olympic gold **medals**. People consider him one of the greatest **athletes** of all time. Usain's world records make him the fastest man alive.

SNAPSHOT

NAME:
Usain St. Leo Bolt

BIRTHDAY:
August 21, 1986

BIRTHPLACE:
Sherwood Content,
Jamaica

TURNED PROFESSIONAL:
2004

OLYMPIC MEDALS WON:
9 gold

CHAMPIONSHIPS:
world championships

FAMILY TIES

Usain St. Leo Bolt was born in Sherwood Content, Jamaica, on August 21, 1986. His parents are Wellesley and Jennifer Bolt. Usain has a brother named Sadiki. His sister is Sherine.

WHERE IN THE WORLD?

Sherwood
Content

Jamaica

CARIBBEAN
SEA

EARLY YEARS

Growing up, Usain led a simple life in Jamaica. His family lived in a house with no running water. His parents owned the grocery store in their small town.

Usain enjoyed playing soccer and **cricket**. By age 12, he was a top **athlete** at his school.

Usain's parents have always been very supportive of him.

STARTING OUT

When Usain started high school, he decided to try track and field. Even though he was good at hurdles and high jump, Usain wanted to focus on **sprinting**.

At age 14, Usain ran in a high school sports **championship**. He won a silver **medal** in the 200-meter race.

When he switched to track and field, Usain found he had a natural talent for sprinting. He needed little training before finding success.

BIG DREAMS

Usain wanted to race against the fastest runners in the world. In 2001, he ran in the Caribbean Free Trade Association (CARIFTA) Games.

There, Usain **competed** against the top **athletes** from the Caribbean Islands. He won a silver **medal** in the 200- and 400-meter races.

In 1991, Carl Lewis (*front*) was the fastest man alive. Eighteen years later, Usain beat Carl's 100-meter record by .28 of a second.

In 2002, Usain's life changed forever. He won the 200-meter race at the World Junior **Championships**. There, Usain, age 15, became the youngest person to ever earn a gold **medal**.

In 2002, Usain did not have to travel far for the World Junior Championships. The event was held in Kingston, Jamaica.

15

ATHENS OLYMPICS

At 17, Usain traveled to Athens, Greece, as a member of the Jamaican Olympic team. Sadly, he had a leg injury and didn't run well in the 200-meter race. Usain did not earn a **medal**.

After the 2004 Olympics, Usain worked hard to improve his strength and speed. His **goal** was to win an Olympic medal.

Usain often wears a cross around his neck. He also prays before each race.

BEIJING OLYMPICS

In 2008, Usain took part in his second Olympics. This time it was in Beijing, China. Usain ran 100 meters in 9.69 seconds. He became the world's fastest man!

Then he won a gold **medal** for the 200-meter race. Usain set a new world and Olympic record in 19.30 seconds. In all, he earned three gold medals!

18

In 2008, Usain was the first man to set world records in the 100-meter, 200-meter, and 4x100-meter relay at a single Olympics.

LONDON OLYMPICS

In 2012, the Olympics were in London, England. The world was eager to see if Usain could set more records. This time, he broke his own Olympic record by **sprinting** 100 meters in 9.63 seconds. In the end, Usain took home three more gold **medals**.

In the 4x100 meter relay, Usain *(left)* led his team to a new world and Olympic record of 36.84 seconds.

Usain *(top left)*, Yohan Blake *(bottom left)*, Nesta Carter *(top right)*, and Michael Frater *(bottom right)* beat their previous relay record of 37.04 seconds.

RIO OLYMPICS

The 2016 Olympics were in Rio de Janeiro, Brazil. The crowd cheered every time Usain walked onto the track. He was the favorite to win all three of his events. And, he did not disappoint his fans! Usain earned three more gold Olympic **medals**.

Usain celebrated his
100-meter race win by
carrying the Jamaican flag.

OFF THE TRACK

Usain's world records have made him famous. He has appeared on magazine covers and TV shows. Usain is known for showing off in front of the cameras.

In 2015, Usain met President Barack Obama in Jamaica. Usain showed the President his famous lightning bolt pose.

Usain was on TV in Daegu, South Korea, during the 2011 World Athletics Championships.

25

Usain is the highest-paid **athlete** in track and field. He **promotes** brands for clothing, shoe, and beverage companies. Usain also owns a Jamaican restaurant called Tracks & Records.

Usain uses his time and fame to help others and to bring awareness to causes. The Usain Bolt **Foundation** helps children earn an education and supplies Jamaican schools with sports gear.

In 2009, Usain traveled to Toronto, Ontario, to meet young runners.

BUZZ

Usain plans to **retire** after the 2017 World **Championships** in London, England. But, many hope he runs in the 2020 Olympics in Tokyo, Japan. Fans are excited to see what's next for Usain Bolt!

Usain loves to take pictures with his fans. Sometimes, he snaps the photos himself!

GLOSSARY

athlete a person who is trained or skilled in sports.

championship a game, a match, or a race held to find a first-place winner.

compete to take part in a contest between two or more persons or groups.

cricket a game played on a large field with bats, ball, and wickets by two teams of 11 players.

foundation (faun-DAY-shuhn) an organization that controls gifts of money and services.

goal something that a person works to reach or complete.

medal an award for success.

promote to help something become known.

retire to give up one's job.

sprinter someone who runs at top speed for a short length. Sprinting is to run at a top speed.

WEBSITES

To learn more about Olympic Biographies, visit **booklinks.abdopublishing.com**.
These links are routinely monitored and updated to provide
the most current information available.

INDEX